JAMESTOWN EDUCATION

# Reading Fluency

## Reader

Level
A

**Camille L. Z. Blachowicz, Ph.D.**

D1280387

JAMESTOWN  EDUCATION

# Reading Fluency

## Reader

Level
A

**Camille L. Z. Blachowicz, Ph.D.**

 **Glencoe**

New York, New York   Columbus, Ohio   Chicago, Illinois   Peoria, Illinois   Woodland Hills, California

JAMESTOWN EDUCATION

# Acknowledgments

Grateful acknowledgment is given to the authors and publishers listed below for brief passages excerpted from these longer works.

from *Tom Jefferson: Third President of the United States* by Helen Albee Monsell. Copyright © 1939, 1953, 1962 by the Bobbs-Merrill Company, Inc. Aladdin Paperbacks, an imprint of Simon & Schuster.

from *Wringer* by Jerry Spinelli. Copyright © 1997 by Jerry Spinelli. HarperCollins Publishers.

from *Clara Barton: Soldier of Mercy* by Mary Catherine Rose. Copyright © 1960 by Mary Catherine Rose. Garrard Publishing Company.

from *Annie Oakley: Young Markswoman* by Ellen Wilson. Copyright © 1958, 1962 by the Bobbs-Merrill Company, Inc. Aladdin Paperbacks, an imprint of Simon & Schuster.

from *Because of Winn-Dixie* by Kate DiCamillo. Copyright © 2000 by Kate DiCamillo. Candlewick Press.

*from* "Clear As Mud" from *Undone! More Mad Endings* by Paul Jennings. Copyright © 1993 by Paul Jennings. Puffin Books, a division of the Penguin Group.

from *The Barn* by Avi. Copyright © 1994 by Avi. Orchard Books.

The McGraw-Hill Companies

Send all inquiries to:
Glencoe/McGraw-Hill
8787 Orion Place
Columbus, OH 43240-4027

ISBN: 0-07-861709-X
Printed in the United States of America.
1 2 3 4 5 6 7 8 9 10  021  10 09 08 07 06 05 04

# Contents

The passages in this book are adapted or taken from the following sources.

# How to Use These Books

The Reading Fluency *Reader* contains 36 reading passages. The accompanying *Reader's Record* contains two copies of each of these passages and includes a place for marking *miscues*.

## What Procedure Do I Follow?

**1.** Read a selection from the *Reader* as your partner marks any miscues you make on the corresponding page in your *Reader's Record*. (A miscue is a reading error. See explanation in How to Use These Books in the *Reader's Record*.) The recorder's job is to listen carefully and make a tick mark above each place in the text where a miscue occurs, and to make a slash mark indicating where you stop reading after "Time!" is called.

**2.** The recorder says when to start and calls "Time!" after a minute.

**3.** After the reading, the recorder

- counts the number of words read, using the number guides at the right-hand side of the passage in the *Reader's Record,* and records the Total Words Read

- writes the total number of miscues for each line in the far right-hand column labeled Miscues. Totals and records the miscues on the Total Errors line

- subtracts Total Errors from Total Words Read to find the Correct Words Per Minute (WPM) and records that score on the Correct WPM line

**4.** Review the *Reader's Record,* noting your miscues. Discuss with your partner the characteristics of good reading you have displayed. Then rate your own performance and mark the scale at the bottom of the page.

**5.** Change roles with your partner and repeat the procedure.

**6.** You and your partner then begin a second round of reading the same passage. When it is your turn to read, try to improve in pace, expression, and accuracy over the first reading.

**7.** After completing two readings, record your Correct WPM scores in the back of your *Reader's Record.* Follow the directions on the graph.

Fiction

# adapted from *The Wonderful Wizard of Oz*

by L. Frank Baum

"My dear friends," said Oz. "Think of me. Think of the trouble I'm in."

"Does anyone else know you're a humbug?" asked Dorothy.

"No one knows it but you four—and me," replied Oz. "I have fooled others a long time. I thought I would never be found out. It was a great mistake to let you into the Throne Room. Usually I will not see even my subjects. They believe I am something terrible."

"But, I don't understand," said Dorothy. "How did you appear to me as a great Head?"

"That was one of my tricks," answered Oz. "Step this way. I will tell you all about it."

He led the way to a small room. It was behind the Throne. They all followed him. He pointed to one corner. There lay the great Head. It was made out of paper. It had a painted face.

"This I hung from the ceiling by a wire," said Oz. "I stood behind the screen. I pulled a thread to make the eyes move and the mouth open."

# Grandmother Spider:
## An American Indian Myth

When the Earth began, there was darkness all around. There was no sun or moon. There were not even any stars. People and animals were confused. They bumped into each other. They could not cook their food because there was no fire.

They heard that there was light in the East. Grandmother Spider said she knew a way to get the light. No one believed her because she was so small. But they let her try. She went to the river and found mud. She made a tiny clay pot and lid. She spun a web that stretched to the other side of the world. She put the pot on her back. She traveled on her web to the East.

When she saw the light, she took a piece of it. She put it in her pot and put the lid on. She returned home. Grandmother Spider opened the lid of the pot. Fire leaped out. Grandmother Spider showed the other creatures how to keep fire safe. Now they could see. Now they could cook their food.

# Obasi's Plan

Fiction

Obasi stepped back and looked at the word he had written in the sand. He had spelled the word *HELP* with parts from his small plane. Obasi had lost his way in flight. Then the plane had run out of gas. He had to land in this lonely, windy desert. The landing was bumpy, and some parts of the plane fell off. He used the largest parts to form the word. Before long, the wind might blow sand and cover the word—and everything.

From far away a low hum grew louder. It sounded like an engine. Was it a plane? Obasi looked up but saw nothing. Could a pilot see the word he had made in the sand?

There! There it was! He waved his arms over his head and jumped up and down. The pilot dipped his wings and went around. "He saw it! He saw it!" Obasi shouted.

The plane disappeared. But now Obasi knew help would come. He was too happy to sit down. So he paced, and then he danced.

**4**

from ***Tom Jefferson:***
***Third President of the United States***

by Helen Albee Monsell

"You can't expect three men to pull a whole house down by themselves."

"It is just a small shed," said Father. "Try it again."

No matter how hard they tried, the shed still stood there.

"I reckon we'll have to get a hammer and knock it down a plank at a time," one man said.

"Wait a minute," said Mr. Jefferson. "I'll try it myself."

He jumped down from his horse, went to the shed, and picked up the ends of two of the ropes. He put them over his back and pulled.

The old shed creaked and groaned. He pulled harder still. Tom heard something crack. His father kept on pulling.

Tom could see his father's muscles knot. Big beads of sweat stood on his forehead. He pulled harder and harder. Then there was another crack. The walls were caving in!

Tom began to shout. There arose a big cloud of dust. The shed had fallen!

Father dropped the rope. He dusted his hands and wiped his forehead.

"You see," he told the men quietly. "It *could* be done."

# Pushing a New Idea

Sylvan Goldman owned a chain of food stores. He knew that shopping could be hard. He'd watch people carry full baskets. So in 1936, Goldman invented a helpful tool. It was the world's first shopping cart.

Goldman wanted to show his idea. He was excited. He was sure that shoppers would use the carts. "Who wants to drag around a heavy basket?" he thought. "Now you can just push a cart with wheels."

At first, the cart idea failed. No one liked them. Women thought the carts lacked style. A lot of men passed them up, too. "A strong man doesn't need a cart," they said.

Goldman did not give up. He had a plan. He hired male and female models. He had them push the carts through the store. Each cart was packed with food. A woman stood by the row of carts. She showed shoppers how to use them.

From then on, the carts were a big hit. The demand for them soared. Today shopping carts are used in food stores everywhere.

# from *Wringer*

by Jerry Spinelli

Fiction

His mother called, "Palmer, hurry. They're coming."

The doorbell rang.

"Palmer!"

He flew down the stairs.

His mother waved him on. "Go, go. It's *your* birthday. *You* invited them."

At the door he turned, suddenly afraid to open it. He did not want to be disappointed. "You sure it's them?"

His mother's eyes rolled. "No, it's my Aunt Millie. Open it."

He opened the door—and there they were! Beans. Mutto. Henry. Three grinning faces. Shoving wrapped gifts into his chest. Storming past him into his house, Beans bellowing, "Where's the grub?"

Palmer stayed in the doorway, fighting back tears. They were tears of relief and joy. He had been sure they would not come. But they did. He wondered if they would give him a nickname. What would it possibly be? But that was asking too much. This was plenty. They were here. With presents! They liked him. He was one of them. At last.

Arms full of gifts, he pushed the door shut with his foot and joined them in the dining room.

# Ellen Ochoa:
## Making Dreams Come True

"I always liked school," says Ellen Ochoa. In school, she loved math and science. She played the flute, too. Ellen was good at many things. What job would she choose?

Ellen was excited about space. She wanted to go. She wanted to be weightless. She wanted to see Earth from space. So she chose to become an astronaut.

Ellen worked hard on her dream. It came true when she was 33. She flew on a space shuttle. She was the first Hispanic woman to go into space.

Ellen had one more dream. She wanted to go to the Space Station. It is a special place in space. Many countries use it. They send astronauts there to learn about space. In 1999, Ellen got her wish.

Ellen is a busy person. But she still makes time to visit schools. She talks to students. She tells them that school is fun. She says to work hard. Ellen tells them that hard work will make their dreams come true.

**Pronunciation Guide**

Ochoa: Ō chō' wə                    astronaut: as' trə nôt'

# Getting a Web Site

So you want to have your own Web site? Well, it's not that hard to do. You just have to follow some simple steps. First, answer two easy questions. Why do you want a Web site? What do you want the site to do?

Next, plan your Web site. What's going to be on it? Do you want pictures, words, and links? Will it be one page or more? Sketch each page on paper. Think *simple.* The site should be easy to use.

Look at the pages you've sketched. You know what Web users are like. You need to get their attention fast. So keep each page short. Get right to the point.

Now you're ready to build the Web site. The easiest way is to find a Web-building program. The program will guide you one step at a time. It will even code your work in HTML. That's the format used to build Web sites.

When you're done, the fun can start. Tell all your friends to visit your new Web site!

**9**

Fiction

adapted from **"How the Camel Got Its Hump"**

by Rudyard Kipling

Camel hated to work. One day Horse came to see Camel. "Come work with me," Horse said.

"Humph!" said Camel. In fact, that is all he ever said. Horse went away.

Next, Dog came by. "Help me do my job," Dog begged.

"Humph!" said Camel, so dog left.

Finally, Ox visited Camel. "Come plow the field with me," Ox said.

"Humph!" snorted Camel.

The animals told Man that they were angry that Camel was so lazy. "You will have to do his part, then," said Man. This made the animals *very* angry. Just then Wise Man came along. The animals told him their problem.

Wise Man went to see Camel. "Why won't you work?" he asked.

"Humph!" grunted Camel.

"Stop saying that!" said Wise Man.

"Humph!" said Camel. Suddenly, a big humph grew on Camel's back. "Now I *can't* work," said Camel.

"Yes, you can," said Wise Man. "You can store food in your humph. In fact, you can work and work and work without stopping to eat." Ever since, Camel has worn a humph, only now we call it a hump.

**Pronunciation Guide**

Humph: humf

from *Clara Barton:*
*Soldier of Mercy*

by Mary Catherine Rose

[Clara] watched David climb the ladder to the top of the new barn. "What a big, strong brother I have!" Clara thought. "How brave he looks standing on that long board so high above the ground."

Suddenly the board broke and David fell crashing to the ground. Everyone ran to help him.

"I'm all right," David said, standing up. "I wasn't hurt."

But later that night David's head began to [hurt]. He had a high fever. When the doctor came, Clara waited outside David's door.

"He won't let anyone come near him," Clara heard her mother say. "Poor boy. He is in such pain."

"Please, Mother," Clara begged. "Let me see David. Let me try to help him."

"All right, child, but only for a few minutes," her mother said.

Clara went into the room. David had always been so strong. Now he lay still. His face was white. His eyes were closed.

The doctor was afraid David would die. But Clara was sure she could make him well.

# Digging Out

The woman started the letter. She wrote the date, March 13, 1888. Then she stopped. She wanted to be careful about what she said. She was worried about her son. She was sure he was worried about her, too.

It was the second day of the blizzard in New York. They had not heard from each other. Phone lines were down. Some newspapers had not gone to press. And she didn't know when the letter would reach him. "Maybe *some* mail is getting through," she thought.

She could tell him what the weather forecast had been. March 12 was supposed to have light snow. But the forecast had been wrong. Twenty inches of snow had fallen. Strong winds were forming drifts as high as 20 feet. There was much danger. Some people were dying.

She looked out the window. Snow and sleet were still coming down.

"I will let him know I am safe," she thought. "For now, that will be enough. And, oh, how I hope he is safe as well."

"My dear son," she began.

## adapted from *Alice's Adventures in Wonderland*

Fiction

by **Lewis Carroll**

"Your hair wants cutting," said the Hatter. He had been looking at Alice with great curiosity. This was his first speech.

"You should not make personal remarks," Alice said. "It's very rude."

The Hatter opened his eyes wide on hearing this. All he SAID was, "Why is a raven like a writing desk?"

"We shall have fun now!" thought Alice. "I'm glad they're asking riddles. I can guess that," she added aloud.

"You think you know the answer?" said the March Hare. "Is that what you mean?"

"Yes," said Alice.

"Then you should say what you mean," the March Hare went on.

"I do," Alice replied. "At least I mean what I say. That's the same thing, you know."

"It's not the same thing. Not a bit!" said the Hatter. "You might just as well say that 'I see what I eat' is the same thing as 'I eat what I see'!"

"You might just as well say," added the March Hare, "that 'I like what I get' is the same thing as 'I get what I like'!"

# 13 Just One of the Herd

⚬⚬⚬

Llamas are cousins of the camel. They are often used to carry loads. Their wool makes a warm cloth. Llamas are friendly. They like being part of a herd.

They also make good guards. No one knows that better than a man named Bailey.

Bailey has a farm in England. He also has a herd of llamas. The llamas' names are Berti, Milo, Horatio, and Felix. They guard Bailey's sheep from foxes and wild dogs.

In the fall of 2003, Bailey went to feed his llamas. He stepped into a hole in the ground and fell. He knew that he had hurt his hip. He crawled to the edge of the road. A woman saw him and called for help.

The llamas formed a ring around Bailey. After all, he was one of their herd. They would not let anyone get close to him. They took turns chasing people off. Who was in charge? They all said Milo was the one. But all's well that ends well. Farmer Bailey got better. And no one was hurt by a llama.

**Pronunciation Guide**

llama: lä′ mə                    Horatio: hə rā′ shē ō′

# The Great Wall of Los Angeles

One day, artist Judith Baca looked at a wall in Los Angeles. It was plain and flat. Baca had a thought. Could the wall be a work of art? She asked if she could paint a large mural on it. She wanted to tell the story of California in pictures. The city leaders said she could.

Painting the mural was a big job. Hundreds of people helped. It took years to plan the pictures. Then it took years to paint them. Many of the painters were students. The work was finished in 1984. It was named *The Great Wall of Los Angeles*.

*The Great Wall* is huge. It's 13 feet high and a half a mile long. It might be the longest mural in the world. The mural shows people of long ago. It shows people of today. Some are famous. Most are not. The pictures show people of many races. They show people of all ages. *The Great Wall of Los Angeles* is one of the city's best-known murals.

**Pronunciation Guide**

mural: my o͞or əl

## adapted from *The Mysterious Island*
by Jules Verne

The hot-air balloon rose 2,000 feet. The five travelers had climbed into the netting. There they clung, gazing down. They had cut everything loose to make the balloon lighter. Nothing could save them now. They had done all that they could do.

At four o'clock the balloon was only 500 feet above the water. A loud barking was heard. "Top has seen something," cried one. Then suddenly one of them shouted. "Land! Land!"

The balloon, which the wind still drove, had gone a long way since daybreak. But the land was still thirty miles off. It would take an hour to get to it. There was a chance the wind would shift.

An hour! The travelers could clearly see the spot that they must reach. They did not know what it was. It might be an island or a country. They did not know to what part of the world the storm had pushed them. But they had to reach this land, no matter what waited for them there.

# Percival Lowell and Planet X

Percival Lowell looked up at the night sky. He liked seeing the moon, big and glowing. He liked the stars, small and bright. But what he liked best was the sky itself. The sky held a secret!

Up there, far from Earth, a planet was hiding. No one had ever seen it. But from his years of study, he was sure it was there. He called it Planet X. And he began to search for it.

Planet X was too far away to find by just looking up. So he studied the sky with his telescope. The telescope made all the stars look big and close! Surely now he would find Planet X. Each night, he looked for it. But each morning, he went home without finding Planet X.

Lowell died in 1916. He never found Planet X. But others thought it was out there, too. Scientists began to look for it. In 1930, they did find it. It was the ninth planet from the sun. The planet was named Pluto.

**Pronunciation Guide**

Percival: pûr′ sə vəl

# Helen of Troy:
## A Greek Myth

There once was a woman named Helen. She lived in Greece. People thought she was the most beautiful woman in the world. Princes from every land wished to marry her.

Helen's father was the great god, Zeus. One day Zeus called on the princes. His voice thundered as he spoke. "I will choose one of you to marry Helen," he said. "But first, you must make a promise. You each must say that you will not harm Helen or the prince she marries." Each prince promised. After all, each one thought he would be chosen.

Zeus chose Menelaus of Sparta. Helen and Menelaus were soon married. They ruled as queen and king of Sparta.

But one prince, named Paris, broke his promise. Paris thought Helen should be his wife. He took her to the city of Troy. Menelaus called the princes to him. His message was, "Get ready for war!"

The Trojan War had begun. It raged on for ten long years. Menelaus and the princes' armies won the war. Helen came back to Sparta. She and Menelaus lived in peace.

**Pronunciation Guide**

Zeus: zōōs          Menelaus: men' əlā' əs

# Eleanor Roosevelt's Answer

The phone rang, and Eleanor answered. She knew the voice. It was Harry Truman, President of the United States. Truman had been Vice President under her husband. But when her husband died, Truman became President.

Eleanor and Truman talked for a short time. Then Truman surprised her. He asked her to be the first to represent the United States at the United Nations. Eleanor said no. But Truman asked her to think about it. She said that she would.

Eleanor did think about it. She also thought of her husband. The United Nations had been his dream. He believed that nations could work together for peace. Eleanor and Truman believed that, too. This was Eleanor's chance. She could help. She could make their dream of peace come true.

Eleanor was afraid she would fail. But she knew she had to try. She said yes. She became the first U.S. delegate to the United Nations. And she did her job very well.

# Chief Black Hawk

Chief Black Hawk was a leader of the Sauk and Fox. The Sauk and Fox were American Indians. They lived in towns in the area that is now Illinois. In the early 1800s, settlers were moving west. They wanted to start towns on the Sauk and Fox's land. Black Hawk's people were told to leave.

The Sauk and Fox moved. But they were not happy. In 1832, some returned. They fought to get their land back. Many of the Sauk and Fox were killed. Some who died were women and children. Black Hawk did not want more people to die. At last, he gave up.

Near the end of his life, Black Hawk gave a speech. He talked about the war. He told how it had hurt the land and his people. He asked the settlers to take care of the land.

"Rock River [Illinois] was a beautiful country," he said. "I loved my towns, my cornfields, and the home of my people. I fought for it. It is now yours. Keep it as we did."

**Pronunciation Guide**

Sauk: sôk

adapted from *Black Beauty*
by Anna Sewell

The first place I lived was a large meadow. There was a pond of clear water in it. Shady trees leaned over the pond. Water plants grew at the deep end. On one side we looked into a plowed field. On the other we looked over a gate at a house. At the top of the meadow was a grove of fir trees. At the bottom, there was a brook.

While I was young I could not eat grass. I lived on my mother's milk. By day I ran by her side. At night I lay down close by her. When it was hot, we stayed by the pond. When it was cold, we had a nice warm shed.

There were six young colts in the meadow. They were older than I was. Some were nearly as large as grown-up horses. I used to run with them. We had great fun. We would gallop round and round the field. Sometimes the play was rough. They would often bite and kick.

## adapted from *Robinson Crusoe*
by Daniel Defoe

I made a cap from goat's skin. The cap had a flap that kept the sun and rain from my neck. My coat was made from the same material. I wore a broad belt around my waist. It was fastened by two strips of leather. I hung a saw and an ax from it on my right side. I attached a pouch for shot on the left side. I had not cut my beard since I arrived.

One day at noon I walked down to a part of the shore that was new to me. What should I see there on the sand but the print of a man's foot! I stared at the print. I could not stir from the spot.

Presently, I dared take a look around me. No one was in sight. What could this mean? I went three or four times to look again. There it was. It was the print of a man's foot. I could see the toes, the heel, and all the other parts. How could it have come there?

# Laura Ingalls Wilder:
## Life on the Frontier

Laura Ingalls Wilder stepped down from the wagon. Almanzo reached up and swung Rose to the ground. The year was 1894. They had moved here from the Dakota Territory. So much had happened. Their son had died. Their crops had been lost to a drought. Their house had burned to the ground. They had come here so they could make a fresh start. Laura looked out over the green Missouri hills. The view filled her with hope.

Laura had lived in the Dakota Territory since she was twelve years old. Her pa staked a claim to some land near a lake. They farmed the land in the summer. In the winter Pa worked in town. They were hard years. They almost starved when blizzards stopped the trains from coming through. Still, that had been her world. That was where she had gone to school. She had become a teacher there, and met Almanzo. One day there would be books about Laura's life on the frontier.

**Pronunciation Guide**

Almanzo: ăl mon' zō

# from *Annie Oakley: Young Markswoman*

Nonfiction

by Ellen Wilson

Now that Annie was close to the cow, it seemed as big as a mountain to her. She lost some of her bravery. Did she dare waken the cow? Then she said softly, "Here, Old Black. Here's some supper for you."

Old Black opened her eyes.

Johnny got ready to run. Annie held her skirt in one hand. In the other she held out some of the fresh grass. "Good Old Black," she said. "Good supper."

The cow glared at the children.

Johnny took a step toward the nearest tree, but Annie stood perfectly still.

The cow looked straight at Annie with her big brown eyes. What would she do next? Annie was ready to run. Then the cow opened her mouth and nibbled the grass.

"Nice Old Black," Annie went on in a quiet voice. "Nice Black, you come home with us." Annie started to back out of the clearing, the grass still in her hand.

Old Black lumbered to her feet. She followed Annie through the trees and took more nibbles from her hand.

# Why Pay Taxes?

We know that we must pay for things we get. If we buy goods, we have to pay for them. If a doctor treats us, we will get a bill. This is a private bill. There are also public bills that must be paid. These bills are paid by the government. The funds come from taxes paid by you and me. One kind of tax is an income tax. Almost everyone pays some kind of tax.

Most of the money from taxes is used to protect us. It pays for police and fire fighters. A large amount goes to schools and libraries. Tax funds pay for roads too. They pay for streetlights and traffic lights. They also pay the people who work for the government.

What if no one paid taxes? The water would stop running. Trash would not get picked up. There would be no police force. Schools would close down. All of us need schools and roads. We need a safe place to live. So we pay for it with taxes.

# Nazar the Brave:
## An Armenian Folktale

Nazar heard of a tiger near the town. He started to run home. People thought that he was running to kill the tiger.

Nazar ran into the forest. He climbed to the top of the tallest tree he could find. Scared to death, Nazar held on. He hoped he would not see the tiger.

Just then the tiger walked by. He chose to lie down under that same tree. Nazar looked down and saw the tiger. He began to tremble. He shook so much that he lost his hold on the tree. Down he fell, right onto the back of the tiger!

Up it jumped, trying to shake off the strange weight. Roaring wildly, the tiger ran out of the forest. Nazar closed his eyes and hung on.

"Look!" cried the people. "Nazar has tamed the tiger." The sight of him gave the people courage. They surrounded the tiger and killed it. Nazar scolded them. "Why did you kill the animal? I was going to keep it for a horse!"

# Escaping from Slavery:
## The Story of William and Ellen Craft

Nonfiction

William and Ellen Craft were enslaved people in Georgia. Ellen's father was white. Her mother was of mixed race. Ellen was so light-skinned that most people thought she was white. William was dark. They married and planned their escape. They soon found that freedom lay at the end of a long road.

Their plan called for Ellen to dress as a white man. Piece by piece, William bought the clothes that she would wear. One night, he cut her hair short. She also put her arm in a sling and a bandage around her throat. They planned to travel to the North on trains and boats. They thought if Ellen looked sick, she would not have to talk with other travelers. William would go with her. He would pretend to be her slave.

In 1848 William and Ellen made their escape. For a time, they lived in Boston. Then they began a new life in England. There, they were safe and free. They did not come back to the United States until 1868. By then, slavery had ended.

## 27

adapted from *The Swiss Family Robinson*

by Johann David Wyss

The next day Fritz and I returned to the ship that was broken on the rocks. First we saved the animals. We attached floats to the cow, the donkey, the sheep, and the goats. Then we threw them into the sea and tied them with ropes to our raft. We loaded the raft with food and other things that had not been spoiled by saltwater. At last we put out to sea.

I heard a loud cry of fear from Fritz. "We are finished! See what a great shark is on its way to us!"

Though pale with fright, Fritz took aim. He shot the fish in the head. It sank at once. When back on shore, we emptied the raft of the things we had brought. The poor beasts were almost worn out. We tended to them and put them to rest on some dry grass.

That night my wife spread a cloth on the top of a barrel. With the knives and forks from the ship, we dined on hot ham and eggs.

# from *Because of Winn-Dixie*

by Kate DiCamillo

"Well," said Miss Franny, "I looked at [the bear] and he looked at me. He put his big nose up in the air and sniffed and sniffed as if he was trying to decide if a little-miss-know-it-all librarian was what he was in the mood to eat. And I sat there. And then I thought, 'Well, if this bear intends to eat me, I am not going to let it happen without a fight. No ma'am.' So very slowly and very carefully, I raised up the book I was reading."

"What book was that?" I asked.

"Why, it was *War and Peace,* a very large book. I raised it up slowly and then I aimed it carefully and I threw it right at that bear and screamed, 'Be gone!' And do you know what?"

"No ma'am," I said.

"He went. But this is what I will never forget. He took the book with him."

"Nuh-uh," I said.

"Yes, ma'am," said Miss Franny. "He snatched it up and ran."

"Did he come back?" I asked.

"No, I never saw him again."

# Spiders

A spider is a small, eight-legged animal. Spiders are best known for the silky threads they spin. They use this thread to catch insects. Many spiders make webs. They use these webs as traps. If you look at a web, you can see the pretty patterns made by the spider.

But some spiders do not make webs. One kind of spider jumps onto an insect. Another spider uses its thread like a fishing line. It swings the line until it catches a bug. Then it pulls up the line to eat its catch.

Spiders are not insects. They belong to a group called arachnids. All these animals have eight legs. None of them has feelers. Mites and ticks belong in this group.

Spiders lay eggs. Some large spiders lay 2,000 eggs at a time. One small spider lays just one egg. Many spiders die after they lay their eggs.

Many people are afraid of spiders. But only a few spiders can hurt humans. In fact, spiders are very helpful. They get rid of many harmful pests.

# 30 Lady Moon:
## A Chinese Legend

*Fiction*

One day long ago, ten suns appeared in the sky. People were frightened. The heat from the suns burned the earth. The lakes and rivers dried up. Crops baked in the fields. The Queen knew she had to do something. She called for her best hunter, Hou-Yi.

"Shoot nine suns from the sky," she said. "Leave just one. If you can do it, I will give you a potion. It will make you live forever." Hou-Yi shot nine arrows. Nine suns fell from the sky. Hou-Yi took his prize. When he arrived home, Hou-Yi gave the potion to his wife, Chang Er.

The next day, Hou-Yi went out to hunt. An evil man came and tried to take the potion from Chang Er. Chang Er drank the potion. She instantly flew into the sky. Worried about her husband, Chang Er landed on the moon because it was close to the earth. From that day, Chang Er has ruled over the moon.

**Pronunciation Guide**

potion: pō' shən

## adapted from *Jack and Jill*

by Louisa May Alcott

Fiction

"Here come Molly Loo and little Boo."

Down the hill came a girl with her hair flying. A small boy sat on the sled behind her. His short legs stuck out. His round face looked over her shoulder like a full moon.

"Molly Loo is the only girl that dares to try this long hill to the pond. I wouldn't for the world. The ice can't be strong yet," said a timid girl.

"Clear the track for jolly Jack!" sang some boys. They had rhymes for nearly everyone. Down came Jack and Jill on a red sled. The boy on it was all smiles. Behind him clung a pretty girl. She had black eyes and hair. Her cheeks were as red as her hood. She waved Jack's blue scarf with one hand as she held on.

"Jill goes wherever Jack does. He can't say no to a girl," said one of the boys slyly. The boy had wished to borrow Jack's red sled. But Jack had refused because Jill wanted it.

# Pow—It's Gone

"I saw a great big shining light," said Betty Barrett. "It hurt your eyes to look at it." Frightened, she rushed to a friend's house. "I felt foolish," she later said. "If I hadn't seen it, I guess I wouldn't have believed it either."

Barrett and her friend went out to look again. This time they saw nothing. The women turned to go. Just then, something blew up. They saw a huge flash of fire. Then it was gone.

What was going on? Where did this ball of light come from? And why did it vanish so quickly? No one knows for sure. But stories like these have been around for a long time.

In 2000, two scientists made a guess. They said that burning silicon might have caused the light. Silicon is found in the soil. The right mix of heat and silicon can cause a ball of heat. If the heat is high enough, it will explode. No one has proved this yet. But bursting balls of light could be real. Couldn't they?

# from "Clear As Mud"

by Paul Jennings

Fiction

I rinsed my mouth out with water from the creek.
I spat and coughed.

The pain was terrible. My tongue started to swell.
I held the mirror up to my face. I stuck out my
tongue to get a good look because I couldn't see it
properly through my cheeks.

I couldn't see it properly through my cheeks?

I couldn't see it at *all* through my cheeks.

A pinkish blush was spreading over my face.
[I could see] eyelids. Lips. A nose. My skin was
returning to normal. I couldn't see my spine. My
skull was covered by normal hair and flesh. My
chin sprouted a dark beard.

I just sat there and watched as the normal color
slowly spread over my body. Skin, lovely skin. It
moved down my neck. Over my chest. Down my legs.

By the next day I was a regular human being.
Not a kidney or lung to be seen. One bite of the
beetle had made me see-through. And another had
cured me.

I could go home. I looked like everyone else again.

# John Henry:
## An American Legend

John Henry was born strong. Even as a baby, he played with hammers. He hammered fence posts. He hammered nails. He hammered huge rocks into tiny stones.

As a man, he worked for the railroad. One day his boss ordered, "John Henry, make a tunnel through that mountain there." So John grabbed his hammer. He banged and banged through the mountain.

Each day, the tunnel grew. But still, his boss said, "John Henry is not fast enough!" So the boss started to use a steam drill.

John Henry declared, "I will die before I let a machine take my job!"

He raced with the steam drill. The mountain shook from his hammer's boom. "On and on," John declared, "I will die before I let a machine take my job!"

Then the race was done. John Henry had won! He wiped his red, wet face and smiled. Then he sank to the ground. The race was too much for his great heart. Now John Henry rests in a grave by the train tracks.

# Fossil Hunter

Mary Anning learned about fossils from her father. Fossils are the hardened remains of plant or animal life from long ago. The Annings lived on the coast of England. The cliffs that rise up from the sea are full of fossils. They were Richard Anning's hobby. He died in 1810 when Mary was 11. He had been poor. He left his family nothing.

Fossils became a source of money for the Annings. They weren't worth much. People liked odd things like these, though. They bought small ones to take home.

Mary had sharp eyes and a good sense of where to look. She was also fearless. Rock slides were a danger. It would have been easy to slip. But she had both luck and skill. She found many animal fossils. Some were new to science. Some had wings. Others had fins like fish.

Mary Anning should have been famous. Scientists often wrote about her fossils. But few scientists gave her credit for her finds. They didn't see her as an equal.

## from *The Barn*

by Avi

For a response he only gaped at me. But I would not give up. I fetched the lamp, lit it, and set it down so we could see each other clearly. Then, once again, I tried: "Father, how *important* is it to *you* that we have a *new* barn? You *must* find a way to *tell* me.

His eyes blinked some, but I wanted more.

"*Show* me how important!" I demanded. "You've got to."

He opened his mouth and made his sounds. But that was nothing new. I shook my head and cried, "I need *more!*"

He shut his eyes. His body tightened. His feet twitched. His fingers fluttered. It was like some strong man preparing to lift a huge load. In fact, what he did was jerk his right hand up. In fairness it was hardly more than an inch. But I could not have read him more plainly if he had written it out.

From that moment on, I was certain I had found the way to bring him back to life: we would build him a barn.